Has No Kinsmen

Has No Kinsmen

poetry

Kimberly Burwick

Black Goat   Los Angeles

HAS NO KINSMEN

Cover art: *BodyCam*, detail by Dennis Potami

Book design by Michael Vukadinovich
Cover Design by Mark E. Cull

The Series Editor thanks
Elias Wondimu and Tsehai Publishers for their assistance.

ISBN: 1-59709-060-3
Library of Congress Catalog Card Number: 2005933592

Published by Red Hen Press

The City of Los Angeles Cultural Affairs Department, California Arts Council, Los Angeles County Arts Commission and National Endowment for the Arts partially support Red Hen Press.

First Edition

Acknowledgements

Grateful acknowledgement is made to the editors of the following publications in which these poems, or earlier forms of the poems, have appeared: *Fence*, *The Florida Review*, *Barrow Street*, *Poetry Wales*, *Hayden's Ferry Review*, *River City*, *nthposition*, and *bigcitylit*.

I would like to thank Chris Abani for his help with the production and editing of this book, and Percival Everett for his introduction.

I am grateful to Eloise Klein Healy, Amy Taylor, Megan Moynihan, Michelle Bigley, Jill Osier, Michael Morse, Erik Steinbauer and Javier Arean for their help with this manuscript.

And thanks, especially, to Kevin.

Contents

IV

Has No Kinsmen

Introduction

This is an introduction to a book of poems. To what extent an introduction is a part of anyone's understanding of a book is a good and timely question. The poems are here to do their work, but the reader's reception of that work is informed by the cover, the biographical information of the author, the weight of the book, the shape of it, the font, the binding and, now, the introduction. I do not see that I am here to convince you to read this book, though I think you should and hope you will. The shape of this volume is challenging and different so I offer this.

Why would a fiction writer offer an introduction to a volume of poems? Perhaps that is not the question. The question is why would you care that a fiction writer introduces a volume of poems? More specifically, why would this particular fiction writer famously unfamiliar with the present world of poetry, woefully unequipped for such an undertaking, be someone to whom you might listen concerning a volume of poems? The answer is simple and not. *Has No Kinsmen* by Kimberly Burwick does not depend on its identification as poetry for meaning.

I am a painter of canvases. I make them to stand in opposition to my fiction in the workings of my own, very private artistic life. I love abstraction, am attracted to it on almost a biological level. So far, in order for me to make meaning in fiction, I have been bound to adhere to some kind of representation, regardless of any experimental elements my work might exhibit. To have the stuff of literary artifice and activity broken down into its constituent parts, whether phonemes, words or sentences and have them reassembled in a way to suggest the quintessence of their meaning is a thrilling prospect. I jealously assert that this is what Kimberly Burwick does in *Has No Kinsmen*.

The shifting form, the use of negative space, stalled and interrupted cadence and even the syncopated release of irony work in themselves to create meaning along with, in opposition to and simultaneously with the abstracted center. Each section offers this startling relationship and the sections together repeat this for the whole.

One of the sadder moments in my life came while I stood at the National Gallery in Washington. I overheard a conversation between a father and his son as they positioned themselves in front of a large Motherwell. It's the old story, but it's mine this time. The father to the boy, "You could do that?"

"Not that big," the boy said. "Could you do that Daddy?"

"Who couldn't?" the father said.

This is sad in too many ways. But the most profound way for me was that the boy was not allowed to stand in silence and wonder about the work. He wasn't free to have the painting make whatever meaning it was going to make for him, even if it turned out to be nonsense, or the thought that he could make that. I have no doubt that the boy was equipped to face the work. The father as well, if not for his mouth.

And so, I will say little. Only that every poem here is a riddle of sorts, but there is no joke. Every space has some purpose, as does every word and every word's position with and against every other word. There is an illusion of fragmentation and also of cohesion and illusion becomes just that. Finally however there is simply a love of words and language. These poems cannot be reduced to their content, but neither can content be in any way understood as mere device. This work is aching to get into the world and mean things. It will.

—Percival Everett
California, 2004

This is *infirmitas*, the breaking
of time from day to day
and from hour to hour,
it is rust and fire
and the salt of the planets
darkness even at noon and
luminaries absent from heaven.

—W.G. Sebald

I

Indication Of The Opening Moments

Wailing has come how the orthodox have come mouths closed eyes closed
consanguinity between them like The Law of Good Continuation
initiating itself in the dark.

The Law of Good Continuation initiating itself in the dark like the rise
and fall of a reflection that reappears on the crest of your midnight
to witness you soaking.

The rise and fall that reappears on the crest of your midnight watching you
the way you watch foam and rainwater flooding the arches of an empty foyer
as if waiting to be photographed.

Foam and rainwater flooding the arches of an empty foyer as if waiting
to be photographed the small pools rising the small blue pools
enormously confusing in their ability to hold you.

The small pools rising the small blue pools enormously confusing
in their ability to hold you the way no woman no man no orphaned child
could hold this rising this swelling this small.

The way no woman no man no orphaned child could hold this rising
this swelling this small or the way dark finds itself against glass that would with wailing
detonate an imagine of these mouths eyes closed holding you.

DE' OBRA NE' CORPI

—so that darkness may leave you   in a room where you see this
—in a room where   something waiting to be clothed   cloaks itself   as if you see this
—after several days motionless,   Rachmaninoff
—at your feet in the room where the suddenness of orbit   deadens
—as if waking could undo   this dream where, separately, someone in shadow draws water
—from a melting body in an April thaw,   while someone is saying
—something about the core temperature   of the room   in Russian, with a degree of lust
—for the body of Rachmaninoff who enters and exits   without a word
—to those caught in sunlight   upon waking

DELLI FUMI DELLE CITTÀ

—A rain that begins with the first letter of your name   a square, then a mass of squares
—A eulogy with fingers in the softest sand, the fingers just shy   of you, me
—Before this house of female rain took in traces of smoke   and pieces of city.

—Before you take the shutter you taste the heritage   of her lips, name the wideness.
—You and this in any city but ours,   you and this
—Or Orpheus   rearranging what would carry us in the name of dark fog.

DELLA GRATIA DELLE MɆBRA

—By memory the muscles this music these steps   the boneless, in Michoacan
—you imitate the garbed, the adorned.   In childhood this midnight is filling with water.

—Wordless: the center   of things
—In this light he'll free himself twice.   This midnight her child with water these steps.

—Pardon this city the sandbar these men.   In childhood these steps the seas are rising.

At Her Feet He Sank

No electrical storm
to illuminate
the cooling, the body
charged with no lilac-pink
blaze but it's own, as he watches
the bifurcated oaks casting amnesty
across the skin that folds
and fastens to the face
that curtains
the sensation of pull.

At Her Feet He Sank II

Only to find
a piece of wing
soaking, the sheer feathers soaking
from the wailing
he heard here, this morning.

At Her Feet He Sank III

As if this were happening inside a navy blue crack
between the crust of midnight and the ultramarine
tier of hours, the phantom of her
loving, the phantom of her
taking in the name
of the river.

In The Vessels Of Wood And Stone

—Imagine him gazing back like that: an angle with fixed legs an angel
—or a child a small child
—waving a child his thin yellow hair a child his fingers his dolls his marionettes
—the things he calls fawns the fawns that carry him
—into blackness into love into June the ceaseless shadows the four hands
—two of them his two of them fixed
—like the legs of this angel his gazing
—on objects all of them heavy with fabric the dead the weight of fresh sunlight.

Congregation

Nearby, they'll be returning,
they'll be strung together,
singular bodies torn,
earth-red hushed
with long necks and heads tilted,
mute spaces between those whines and drones
like the sound of these photographs,
or the sound of you
on trains I cannot recognize.

Notes On The Photography Of James Casebere

Asylum 1994
In the hollow your hair this pendulum these vibrations
—in time, the occupant—torn asunder.

Tunnels 1995
Behind me below me above me—all-night singing.

Arches 1985
The reason you unclasped five of your fingers and laid them
instead—upon my face.

Hospital 1997
Some said loft you called it—a wish.

Taking The Waters

He's trapped a piece of the living in his hands   from this distance she can hear the emergency.
Agony, this crowd in winter then laughter   cast back.
Softer, human these sounds your breath into water   forgive me.

From this distance, testimony   these hands this winter
these waters this minute your hair, soaking.   This ends again and again.
His rhythm this winter these salts those lines   that sea-bird, disjointed.

Emptiness, the taste of salt   upon her hands.
In Sanskrit   these waters this memory my god this ocean
is unattended.

Preparations

from The Nei P'ien of Ko Hung

1

Flowers of Cinnabar

Alchemy—the sun-bathed widow making arrangements at the door.
Lake salt, arsenolite, oyster shells—the rough rain not pounding, but tender
on this sodden stretch.

Medicine, rough rain, these feet. *Red bole, soapstone, white lead*—
your imaginary steps, walking the sodden stretch.
The verb: preparing, steps on steps.

When a peasant acquires a ceremonial red bow, he uses it to hunt birds.
In these preparations you find me, feral,
hunting the sodden stretch.

2 and 3
Divine Cinnabar

The metallic turn, the lunge toward preparations.
She carries the salad dressing,
refrigerates the weeping greens,
smears the soles of her feet.

Oral, abandoned. Arrangements lunge past.
Preparing the golden infinitives: to cross, to step.

Thirty-six days of resealing every unwritten word.
This wood and green beneath my feet.
Studying the hemlock, the poisonous smear.

4

Reverted Cinnabar

Not here, but the 320 AD of China,
I obey you obeying phoenixes.

Medicine: the hemorrhaging word.

If I can be *drawn out or stretched like a skin*,
I will prolong my mouth, taste the dead.

5

Gustatory

Refrigeration—the weeping greens.
The lust of preparing the plate.
Thirty days of walking around the yard.
My knotted hair tangled, torn.

A Chinese August: drips, watering the attentive root.

What comes back in your place is something slain
by the sun on the fractured deck.
Something unlike heat.

6
Refined

The interruption of words: unlearned, elegant.
Not a phoenix now, but a red-winged blackbird.
Mercurial, fluid.

Only on hearing thunder and lightening
does one realize the weakness of signal drums.
When a woman acquires a husband, she uses him to hunt birds.

In these preparations you find me, widowed,
preparing the sodden stretch.

II

Has No Kinsmen

Now, from this gurney, the coronal sutures snapping
one by one,
the cruel unlearning of the word
Hiroshima
as beads of sweat magnetize as I raise my head to say
your first name for the first time
again. The temptation to be packed in and taken
like the others,
finger to finger,
iron to iron the spoil
of urine and hard candy corroding
the stitches of your youngest brother's pants
at a time when the autumnal blush of winter's arrival
meant nothing.

The first day I spoke your first name—morning.
Lovesickness and recovery, the warm and steady English breeze until softly,
my illness for the patterns
your eyes choose when unfocused
while speaking of temperature gradients
on the North Ridge of Everest, the snowpack
still heavy from the warm and wet event
earlier. You said, Mallory
couldn't have reached
the summit alone, without Irvine,
unless the perfunctory footstep
onward was enough to save a man
from falling away, and with that word,
away—Sara.

Scarcely a difference between what they took
with them and what blew through
the second story window.
The eyes that shuttle us
back and forth across the barren and destroyed
matter, until we reach
the year of this German window,
until we reach the distant flutter
of Django Reinhardt's fourth and fifth digits the color
of bronze, curled
from overexposure
to smoke and blaze,
curled the same year
you unlearned the word—*Manouches.*

From this gurney, photographs
the nurses take of me,
the small tasks divided
into quadrants, the lower half
of my left arm, which is not an arm,
but a wing when set
to music.

Midnight's iron
gaze. From this gurney,
that English morning—cobalt—a tenderness now
flayed. Sara, before becoming
Sara your wife. The bare of her shoulder if never
before than this minute, mechanically
touching down.
Reconnaissance, a letter traveling the length of that epic
summer, 1924, a letter
making its way across the Himalaya
to that green patch of English earth.
The earth that would,
if only for a moment,
rise up at the feet of Ruth Mallory
and gently command this new widow, as before—*pour*
out your pity, dearest, pull it up from you deepest wells—
smelling that sodden stretch beneath her, smelling this
race of heroes, the Tibetan missive
fluttering like a tattered white
flag in the small
of her classical hands.

From this gurney,
the privilege
of those cerulean eyes.
The steady decline of men, extermination amidst these winter sports.
Your younger brother's larynx
as he is unpacked, the space between them as he begins
to hum—
Django's Tiger—
while being undressed and taken
to the small shower house
where he will dance
to the flutter
of human wings
collapsing.

From this extended infancy
the wings of a child raised at home
a hundred years.
The small tasks
divided into epochs,
the perfunctory footstep
onward until Hesoid's golden race, untouched
by work
or sorrow, gives way
to silver and this experiment,
humanity, begins
as we acquire
the ability to perform
sacrifice.

III

Inside Ayatari's *Moon*

Try finding water.
Try metal. Touch the tongue to metal, find it awful.
You are only a man undressing
who has become dangerous. Try the ice
that creeps up
each tree and put yourself against it: the boneless gate of blood
moving the heart: the single line you are,
the long body you are not, your shoulders still twisting.
If another man finds you this way he will not see the stepladder
you have become.
He will see only you, the moon: the both of you
coiled, in wind in want and vapor and he will toss
the last of the cones
into water, if water, and ask again if echo
is not a way station.
If in the evening the bridge does not become.

Ice Maiden

Always the world turned lighter this way—
Wind ripping into the lesser doldrums.
Wind, or a photograph
of someone's mother, in shadow,
breathless the way we get lost
in nightmares of arid regions or geometrical progressions—
Calling out names
of mountains.

Hides

Variations on Antony Gormley's Land, Sea and Air II

It became the place we left one after the other:
three fiberglass bodies
in solid January light:
the easy snows departing,
the impression
of arriving
weightless on the steel wings
of repair back when repair was another
body: sea-green
and flowering expecting gates salt in other
words: bells

Fibonacci

Abusing even the reconstruction of it.

The way memory shifts from china back to porcelain.
Wilted greens dark and stranded on the plate.
Moving away from it the way sorrow leaves the eyes
before returning.

I fear the piles of people taken for luggage taken for photographs—art
blowing off Charles Bridge. I fear the memory of it, the husk
of a disappearing image.
A German child fading from the glossy print, fading
and fading the closer you come to the event long past.

So that every time it is rewritten, it is rewritten with the assaulted
consummation of it. Like the sex that happens again, and again.
The pleasure of what we continue to see in the reproduction
of the event that casts the image of two naked selves: attached, contagious.

When it is rewritten, it is written mathematically.

Squat memory speak cast event disappearing contagious pleasure.
Memory cast event speak pleasure.
Long white pleasure.
Long disappearing.
Event.
Event.

So that every time it is rewritten, it is rewritten with pleasure.

Painting At Court

When he comes to the weavers with his kerosene lamps
he can not imagine what was woven
or who was speaking, spreading over
the reproduction—*Las Hilanderas.*

Velázquez's women: timely, molten.
Slippage.
Slaves to dusk.

He'll not remember this, will not be forced to remind himself
of the normalcy of fissure.

Things she must beg for then enjoy:
wideness, the innocuous drift,
a woman to help her with weaving.
A blue gown.

He's in love not with her, her hideous web,
but the ladle of her, her widening pools.
He'll study the reproduction, the monument of her shifts.

Undressing what haunts him until the hurt becomes his own
monument shaking in the steady sway of them—weaving, washing.

Velázquez's women: the brawny breath, a private viewing.
Painted, chained to these sheaves,
these pipes and valves.

On Meeting The Seventh Father Of The House

When the child hears it, he imagines first a swivel then a landing of leaves,
the way a ghost hurls a still mass into a room,
leaving it to settle among the living.
He imagines a Norwegian loneliness as the echo
of a heavy boot lifting.
Imagines hunger. Whining.

The infinitesimal plea disguised as pleasure.
Not the way a boy, but an aging man groans
for the wing-beat of long legs locking and unlocking the Lapland.

Not the boy who wakes to find he has erupted, but the echo
of the boy's eruption entering room after room after room.
The swivel of himself steeping the draft of intrusion.

The landed leaves rising up again—
corporeal, bodies without bodies,
hurling themselves onto the living.

Earthenware More Porous Than Metal, Absorbs Particles Of The Flesh

The morning I left you found
photographs, *Seeing the Earth*
from 80 Miles Up. German V-2 rockets in White Sands,
New Mexico.

October 1950. National Geographic's faded pages
halved by nine AM
glare from the bay window where you are holding
my photograph. Thin yellow hair
and dust that had risen
long before the shutter
snapped.

Furniture that ruins wood when it is not carried but dragged
into the center of a unoccupied room. Grooves, coins,
pages stuck together from the evening we braised
quail.

One fifth of the time it took me to find sand
you crossed the living room, lit matches, launched fire
on a colony of ants.

Modigliani, And The Photograph Of A Jury-Ordered Pakistani Rape

Tens of thousands
of ways to say
I never heard
that nude figure
moan or wail.

Ensemble

This, or you through glass before hearing it—
Before needs, stillness, nearness, loudly
because the shapelessness of hush
never reaches you.

IV

Standing Stones

The way a Norwegian folk tale trumpets a wedge of light
so that upon leaving what you've left
is an invocation or a piece of sea glass
where a dovekie lands in the shallow
to find that his companion has flown
and St. Petersburg
is on fire again.

Standing Stones II

I visit you first
in your second sorrow, where you are feeding rice
to a bantam bird
in the clutches of a Cathedral, a citadel
built of smoke and ice and the bones of a piano
whose marbled knuckles
could have been human.

Standing Stones III

Across the Atlantic, I was wearing my Canadian coat.
You stood convex in the convex light
the way a Norse god waiting for sun
covets half the sky by bowing
on your doorstep to say, "the pianist,
yes, the pianist has died and the dovekie
has left for St. Petersburg
this morning."

Loft

Through blackness—
A city, this island, these dolls.
Spiral stairs he'll climb to where she is lying
facedown and breathing in clean white linen.
She's like the adopted he'll think but say, Soho.
Like the kidnapped but he'll say, kimono.
Like the recently deceased but she'll hear, Slovenia.
Slovenia.

Tactile And Away

Indirectly, the anguished—
the heaviness
of the beautiful.
The way a logarithm disorders a forest with a violence
so gentle you begin to prefer it.
No less taboo
than flesh, the inertia
of childhood the inertia of that black stone
rising from memory, rolling over
the union of the ascending aorta
like an exodus from silence.

Healing In His Shadow

Until a pair
of voices choked with rainwater
recover on your signal, rising
to fall together
as though dying together would make the event less or more severe.
"A pair of wasted legs," you wept
on a marbled-torso
in another woman's garden, "are rather like this."
I was coming close to believing your shadow
had splintered like Masaccio's painted diagonals,
the agonizing verticals
of loveless loving, Saint Peter
on the covered colonnade
where even a pheasant, naked with dying,
dipped in your shadow might recover
its wings, its inclination
to graze the vanishing
light.

Coordinates From Compositions In Blue

La Vie / Verklärte Nacht

1.
As if signaling a human
concern, the Tyrolean wall clock,
chiming at intervals
of two and three-quarters.
As if signaling could cut
the blue frost from
the suggestion that, finally, this is love
by miasma and metronome.

2.
The forest where by cello—a man,
and shamefully, by viola—
a woman. Two pizzicato figures
between despondency
and a rich blue frost.
Three-quarters of her love
for the illegitimate child
she bears.

3.
Footfall, the length of a woman's days—
the measure of her steps between two
am and quarter to three. Picasso
like a hawk above this axis
of sorrow and suggestion,
watertight, without a tear
for the abandoned figures
moaning from where he is pointing.

4.
In every hour, the curvature
of seconds it takes to reveal yourself,
the air behind you, the interval
of moans abandoned, Schoenberg's
phantom blue frost hanging,
instrumentally,
from the boughs
of every living tree.

Stammer

Give me the muscle I will need to show
them I need to know the difference I need to
say what lives in the distance can wait and I
will be there when I finish my winter-sleep
though I know that metal polished with dark
is what makes the lilacs turn give me some
form of that flower cut back give me a house
if it takes a house.

Proof

No and yes to that Italian darkness.
South of here she is wearing a dress.
I am wearing that dress.
No and yes inside the cloth.
I am burning that cloth.
Completing that hiss, I am standing in sand.
It is strange that I should see you
as a pile of greens.
I am feeding that pile
with her waist-long hair.
The black hair turns white.
I am finished with the blood-red sound.

Palmovka

Those damn men clean the dark in that city
dark until Easter dark when I see them
in line for fish dark when I ask the sun
for more than what it is
I see that I am washed with that death
pleased with what darkness does to that river
so dark its will moves the other fish down
I ask one man who says it hurts
he says it soft like this just like this.

Untitled

A yak breathing in the cold stays far
but looks back. Even at noon
you think there must be three names
for that roaring hole
in the wet earth we eat.

Vaulted Arc With Violin

Largo ma non tanto in D minor

It's worse than having a memory,
awake and measuring the depraved, local hour
of his departure.
Measuring the convex, the postponed—
the vaulted arc of a whisper's flight leaving the mouth for the door.
Measuring the deep swell of leaving the lost to the flanking of shadows,
measuring the time you heard a single sound from an empty room,
a suitcase against the stain of violins in your head,
against the dead white sheet,
unsure if the temptation to transmit what was
fragrantly estranged to what is foul, forthcoming
might send you off collecting
things: angles, instruments
photographs of corners.

Adagio in E major

You've lost something someone else has
brought him: alarms, flasks
paintings of the naked.
You return with less than the unknown.
Before longing.
Five of your ten fingers against him,
the other five calculating
the number of times you've actually made love
not at once, but in pieces.
The first half of the first time and the time just before
the last when you could hear the last
traveling from the near future.

Andante in A minor

If not against what remembers you
how you remember him or what was in his suitcase,
than against the black swell of the contained
thrust toward the beautiful.
Not against the regular constellations
but the lowest sound that stains the room
and the room that stains the memory.
The present on the corner
of the old Russian sewing machine—
a pocket watch in pieces.

Biographical Note

Kimberly Burwick was raised in Massachusetts, and has lived in the Czech Republic and Western Wyoming where she began writing and mountaineering. She holds degrees from the University of Wisconsin and Antioch University. Her poems have appeared in *Fence*, *The Literary Review* and other journals. Currently, she teaches at the University of Connecticut.